She
Persisted

....

CLARA LEMLICH

....

—INSPIRED BY—

She Persisted

by Chelsea Clinton & Alexandra Boiger

. . . .

CLARA LEMLICH

. . . .

Written by
Deborah Heiligman

Interior illustrations by
Gillian Flint

PHILOMEL

PHILOMEL BOOKS
An imprint of Penguin Random House LLC, New York

First published in the United States of America by Philomel,
an imprint of Penguin Random House LLC, 2021

Visit us online at penguinrandomhouse.com.

Library of Congress Cataloging-in-Publication Data is available.

Printed in Italy
GFV

HC ISBN 9780593115718
10 9 8 7 6 5 4 3 2 1
PB ISBN 9780593115725
10 9 8 7 6 5 4 3 2 1

WRZL

Edited by Jill Santopolo.
Design by Ellice M. Lee.
Text set in LTC Kennerley.

⁓ *For* ⁓
Clara's grandchildren and
all who fight for justice

She
Persisted

....

Dear Reader,

As Sally Ride and Marian Wright Edelman both powerfully said, "You can't be what you can't see." When Sally Ride said that, she meant that it was hard to dream of being an astronaut, like she was, or a doctor or an athlete or anything at all if you didn't see someone like you who already had lived that dream. She especially was talking about seeing women in jobs that historically were held by men.

I wrote the first *She Persisted* and the books that came after it because I wanted young girls—and children of all genders—to see women who worked hard to live their dreams. And I wanted all of us to see examples of persistence in the face of different challenges to help inspire us in our own lives.

I'm so thrilled now to partner with a sisterhood of writers to bring longer, more in-depth versions of these stories of women's persistence and achievement to readers. I hope you enjoy these chapter books as much as I do and find them inspiring and empowering.

And remember: If anyone ever tells you no, if anyone ever says your voice isn't important or your dreams are too big, remember these women. They persisted and so should you.

Warmly,

Chelsea Clinton

CLARA
LEMLICH

TABLE OF CONTENTS

....

·······························

Burning to Read

Clara Lemlich had a fire inside her—a fire for justice, for fairness, for equality. When she saw something wrong, she spoke up. Clara's voice was beautiful and strong, smart and loud. Clara's voice and actions changed the world.

Because of where and when she was born, this was not easy. She *needed* that fire!

Clara Lemlich was born in 1886 to a religious Jewish family in Gorodok, a small village in

Ukraine, which was then part of Russia. In that time and place, girls were supposed to behave and keep quiet. They were not considered equal to boys. And Jewish people were not considered equal to non-Jewish people. In fact, Jews were in constant danger of being killed in attacks called pogroms. Russian leaders supported these pogroms.

Fortunately, for most of Clara's childhood, her family was unharmed. Clara had an older sister, Ella, and four brothers. Her parents owned a small grocery store. Clara's father was a scholar. He studied Jewish books all day. Her mother took care of the children and the house, cooked the meals, and ran the store.

Clara and Ella helped their mother with her work while their four brothers went to school. Clara really wanted to go to school! But only boys went to the yeshiva, the Jewish school. So she asked to go to the village school, where she could learn Russian and other subjects. But the village school refused to let her attend because she was Jewish.

At home, Clara's family spoke and read only Yiddish. Her parents allowed no Russian books, in protest against the Russian rulers. Clara understood, but the books she wanted to read were in Russian. She was *burning* to read novels and history, books about the great world outside their little village. She figured out a way.

Clara made friends easily, and had many—Jewish and non-Jewish. She learned folk songs from her non-Jewish friends, and made a deal with some of her older Jewish friends who knew Russian. She taught them the songs, and they taught her how to read Russian. And they gave her books. Clara knew her parents didn't approve, so she hid the books and read in secret.

She read late at night when everyone else was asleep. She read when she was supposed to be doing chores. Once when she was at the stream washing clothes, she got so caught up reading, she

forgot to go home. Her mother wondered why the laundry took her so long!

Clara read and read and read.

Then one day, her father found her stash of books hidden under a pan in the kitchen. He threw them into the fire!

All of Clara's books, burned to ash.

But that didn't stop Clara for long. She knew she couldn't change her father's mind, but she persisted! She did what she *could* do—she earned money to buy more books. She secretly sewed buttonholes in tailor shops. (Her parents didn't want her to work yet.)

She hid her new books in the attic of their house. That's where she did most of her reading, often on Saturday afternoons, while the rest of the family was napping.

One Saturday, her next-door neighbor happened to look through the window and see her perched on a wooden beam, reading a book.

She begged him not to tell her parents.

Not only did the neighbor not tell, he gave her more to read! And not just books, either, but pamphlets about different kinds of government, and essays about ways to live. Clara read how people could make a difference in the world.

When she grew up, Clara would be one of those people. But first she needed more money for more books.

CHAPTER 2

New Worlds

Clara earned more money by writing letters for women who never learned to write. These letters were to relatives who had left Russia and moved to America. Many Jews were leaving their town because of the danger of pogroms. And then, in 1903, there was a terrible pogrom right near where Clara and her family lived.

Clara's parents knew it was no longer safe to stay in their home. Ella had already left and was working in New York City. She sent money to help bring the rest of her family to America.

In 1904, Clara, her parents and brothers boarded a ship. But when they were examined, Clara's father was told he wouldn't be allowed into America because his eyes were infected.

Clara, full of fire, yelled at the official: "If you don't let him come with us, I will throw myself into the ocean!"

Her father did not get on the ship. He stayed back so his eyes would heal. Even though she didn't win that battle, Clara showed that when she was passionate about something, she would speak up. She was not scared to stand up to anyone—even a person in power.

The ship arrived in New York Harbor, sailing past the Statue of Liberty. On a brass plaque at the base

of the statue are lines from Jewish poet Emma Lazarus. They welcome people from other lands, immigrants to America, assuring them a place of safety and freedom:

"Give me your tired, your poor,

Your huddled masses yearning to

breathe free."

They had arrived in America! Some people said that everyone in America was rich, that the streets were paved with gold. Was it true?

Like most immigrants coming from Europe at that time, Clara and her family entered the country through the Ellis Island Immigration Station, carrying all of their belongings with them. Once they were allowed in—after being examined to make sure they weren't sick—they made their way to their new home on the Lower East Side of New York City, near where Ella lived.

Clara saw the streets weren't paved with gold. But the cobblestone streets were teeming with life: peddlers pushing carts holding fruit and vegetables, clothing and kitchen goods, fabric and hardware. There were people from many different countries pushing those carts, and walking across the streets in front of horse-drawn carriages. Trolley cars carrying many passengers rolled past them all. What a bustling new world they had come to!

This world felt full of possibilites. From all her reading, Clara had strong opinions. She felt that everyone had the right to live a good life—with plenty of food, a safe job with good pay, a nice place to live, love, happiness, and time for music, art, and fun. Everyone deserved that, no matter their religion, their race, their language, or the color of their skin. She believed this was possible in America. If you worked hard, you should be able to have a good life and make your dreams come true.

Clara had big dreams. She would go to school and learn all she could. She would become a doctor. She wanted to start right away.

But when her father arrived a week later, his eyes healthy, he had trouble finding work. Many places preferred to hire young people, mostly girls, whom they could pay much less money for long hours and hard jobs. With her father not able to find work, what were they to do? The family needed money to live, so Clara had to put aside her dreams of school.

Two weeks after landing in America, she went to work. She followed in Ella's footsteps and got a job in a factory that made women's blouses, called shirtwaists. Clara already knew how to sew, but

this was certainly not her dream. She still wanted
to become a doctor. Though that would never be,
the job at the shirtwaist factory would shape her
destiny. Through this job, she would find a different
way of taking care of people. She would discover a
new dream.

·····························

All Fired Up

Clara worked very hard at the shirtwaist factory, seven days a week, from sunrise to sunset every day but Saturday, when she got out at 4:30. But she still wanted to learn. So after her long day at the factory, she would stop at a milk depot, where milk was sold for a penny a glass—and then go to the New York Public Library. She had discovered a branch near her that had many novels in Russian. She read and read, just like back home.

The more she read, the more she wanted to read—and learn. Soon she found a free school, where she could learn English and other subjects. Often she wouldn't eat the dinner plate her mother left her until 11:00 at night. She'd sleep for a few hours before getting up again to go to work.

Clara learned at her job, too. At first she did simple sewing, but she was very good, so she quickly moved up to become a draper. Being a draper took skill—she studied a designer's pattern, then took the fabric, cut it, and molded it over a tailor's dummy. Those pieces would be sewn to make a shirtwaist. That job paid more, but still not very much.

Clara worked in a few different factories as she moved up to draper, and as the months went by she got angrier and angrier at the way they were run. She later wrote, "I think the women who buy and wear the beautiful clothes do not know how it is for the girl who makes them—what conditions she has—or they would care and try to help her."

She described the typical factory: There were three hundred girls crammed into a space much too small for them. To make more money, the bosses put in more machines and more workers, taking away tables for the girls to eat their lunches.

The workers were given lunches—and only half an hour to eat them. They had to wait in line and some might not get their lunches until 12:15 and then have to be back at work at 12:30, as soon as the bell rang. So they ate right next to their machines, but that was risky: if you spilled food on the fabric, you had to pay for it. And if it happened twice, you would be fired.

Like most workers, Clara got paid by the piece. (She kept track of her pieces in a small ledger book so she could be sure she was paid the right amount.) The more pieces you made, the more you got paid, so the girls worked as fast as they could. Sometimes too fast—a finger might get caught in a needle. If you got blood on the fabric, you had to pay for it. If that happened twice, again, you'd be fired.

The girls made so little money, less than men and boys, but the bosses looked for ways to pay them even less. Clara wrote, "If you are three minutes late, you are locked out for half a day and lose half a day's pay. The working-girl . . . needs every cent she can earn; she can't afford to lose a day's wages!"

The factories were dirty, and there was not

enough time or space for the workers to wash their hands before or after they ate. "There is only one sink to wash your hands—in all the factories I was in, there was just one sink—and all the girls crowd

there. The boss gives three towels a week for three hundred girls. You should see that towel at the end of the week! There are only two toilets, and these are cleaned but once a week."

In winter the factories were heated from a coal stove in the middle of the floor. The ashes were emptied onto the floor every morning, but cleared away only once a week, adding to the filth.

Clara found it all unbearable: the machines hissing, the foreman—the man in charge—yelling, the terrible conditions. A fire of rage sizzled inside her. She had to make it better. But how?

CHAPTER 4

A Fire in Her Mouth

Clara knew she couldn't change the factories by herself. The people who ran the businesses had much more power than she did. But if she could convince others to join her fight, together they would have more power. She learned about unions: workers who band together to help each other and to ask their employers for better pay and working conditions.

Clara helped form a union for the waistmakers

in New York City, the Waistmakers' Local 25. It would be part of the International Ladies' Garment Workers' Union. Up until then, the ILGWU was mostly men—even though most of the workers were women! Men thought women were not tough enough to strike. To strike means leaving work, not getting paid, and spending hours marching outside, chanting, asking for what you want.

Clara knew women were tough! She used the fire inside her, her great speaking voice, and her lively personality to convince her co-workers to join the union. Her boss fired her. But that didn't stop Clara! She persisted. She got another job and talked to her new co-workers. She stood on street corners and talked to workers as they left their jobs for the day. She told them that they deserved higher pay and shorter hours. *You should have a*

clean place, enough time to eat, she'd say. "To the bosses, the girls are part of the machines they're running," she said. She knew it wasn't right; the workers must strike. She convinced the workers at her new factory to walk out. The boss was furious. He sent tough guys to scare them on the picket line. He sent the police.

Clara got arrested seventeen times.

But still she persisted.

The boss got angrier. One day, after work, Clara heard footsteps behind her. She turned and saw two men, the tough guys from the picket line. One was a burglar, the other a boxer. Clara, only five feet tall and in a long skirt, could not escape or fight them off. The men grabbed her quickly and attacked. They punched her so hard, they broke her ribs. The men ran away, leaving her bleeding on the sidewalk.

But that didn't stop Clara! She made her way to her sister's—she didn't dare let her parents see her like this! Ella took care of her until she was healthy enough to go back out again. Clara showed the workers her bruises and said this was why the union was so important.

All over the Lower East Side of New York

City, people heard Clara. Ten weeks later, thousands more did.

Monday November 22, 1909, was a cool and rainy day in New York City. The weather didn't stop thousands of people from crowding into Cooper Union's auditorium for a meeting about working conditions in New York City factories.

Union leaders gave speeches. Everyone agreed that conditions in shirtwaist factories were terrible. Male union workers said the bosses should treat the workers better. But, those were just words. Clara wanted them to call a general strike. If workers from all the factories went on strike at once, they could have power to change working conditions in all the shops. But none of the speakers called for a general strike.

Clara sat in the audience frustrated. After two hours, she could not stay quiet any longer.

"I want to say a few words," Clara yelled out in Yiddish. The newspapers the next day described her as a "wisp of a girl." She was a woman, not a girl, and there was nothing delicate about her!

Looking back, she said, "Ah, then I had a fire in my mouth!"

When people saw it was Clara Lemlich who had spoken, they yelled out to let her up on the stage. "I have listened to all the speakers," Clara said from the podium. "I have no further patience for talk." She declared that she was

a worker, that she had been suffering all that they had described. Why should men—who get higher wages—be the ones to decide? "I move that we go on a general strike."

The crowd cheered, stamped their feet, waved their hats, scarves, handkerchiefs.

STRIKE! STRIKE! STRIKE! STRIKE!

The next day, workers went to their jobs as usual. But at 9:00 a.m., thousands of shirtwaist makers in New York City left their machines and walked out. Most of them were women and girls.

It became known as the Strike of the Twenty Thousand, though the number who walked out would reach thirty thousand by the end. It was the largest strike of women in the history of the United States.

CHAPTER 5

She Persisted!

The strike lasted for months, and Clara was one of the main people who kept it going. She marched on the picket line at 6:00 in the morning. Then she left to convince more people to join the union. The membership grew from eight hundred to more than twenty thousand. Clara also made speeches to raise money. Often she didn't go to bed until past midnight.

The strike was rough on the workers. Bosses

hired people to taunt them, and they got the police to arrest them. But that didn't stop Clara or the other strikers. They persisted! And it worked. By March, most of the factories where workers had gone on strike signed contracts with better working conditions, higher pay, and shorter hours.

And there was an even bigger win. The strike proved to everyone what Clara already knew: Women are tough. They can lead strikes. Watching what happened in New York City, women all over the country went on strike, too. Clara had made a huge difference. But she knew there was more work to do.

Two years after the strike, a terrible tragedy occurred at the Triangle Shirtwaist factory, another factory in New York City. The Triangle bosses had not signed a contract with the union. They continued to treat their workers badly. And when a fire broke out one day, the women and girls couldn't escape because they had been locked in. Clara's cousin worked there. She survived, but like so many, Clara knew girls and women who died. Of the 500 who worked there, 146 died. This terrible tragedy made many people realize how much more change was still needed to make sure workers were safe.

Clara persisted. She kept speaking out—and working. Bosses didn't want to hire her, so she gave a fake name. When they figured out who she was, they fired her. But she persisted. And then she got a very important job as a factory inspector, helping to make sure the workers would be safe.

But Clara knew that for women to have all the rights they needed, they had to be able to vote, which at that time they weren't allowed to do in most of the United States, including New York. So she joined the fight for women's suffrage, the right to vote.

In 1912, a New York State senator said women shouldn't have to vote because they already have too much to do. Clara had a few words to say about that!

Women "are here and we are here to stay," she

wrote. "We will have to toil. We want a chance to make better laws under which we are to live." Some women finally won the right to vote in the United States in 1920.

On the first day of 1913, Clara got married. Joe Shavelson was a rebel and a rabble-rouser, too. The two shared a passion for opinions, fighting for rights, and making a better world. They had three children: Charlie, Martha, and Rita.

Clara stopped working to take care of the children, but she didn't stop speaking out and organizing.

When meat prices were too high, she organized the women in her neighborhood to boycott butcher shops and stop buying meat. The meat boycott was successful, and prices were lowered again. She did the same when bakeries hiked up

the price of bread. She stood outside bakeries in her neighborhood and told people not to shop there.

She watched as landlords raised the rent on their tenants so high they couldn't afford to pay. She fought them, too. And when people were evicted from their apartments because they couldn't pay the high rent, she organized neighbors to help the tenants put their furniture back in the apartments!

Clara became well known in her neighborhood of Brighton Beach, Brooklyn, as a woman who persisted. She had a strong, powerful walk, a strut, and a real style. Whenever she went out to speak or to join a protest, she made sure she put on lipstick and a nice hat. She advised other women to dress well, too. *If you dress badly*, she told them, *the police will pick you out and arrest you.*

Clara protested against racism. She marched to get hungry people fed. She even ran for office (on the Communist Party ticket), and though she didn't win, the race gave her the opportunity to talk about what she believed in: a good life for everyone.

....

CHAPTER 6

What Would Clara Do?

Clara had strong opinions. She was never afraid to speak out. She put her opinions and her causes before everything, even her children sometimes. They had opinions about that.

Charlie, the oldest, followed in his mother's footsteps, speaking out and protesting from a very young age. He even got arrested during a march against police brutality when he was a teenager. He grew up to be a union leader, fighting for longshoremen and others in the maritime industry. He was well known as a fighter for social justice.

Martha often wished she had a different mother. She'd walk home from school with a friend only to see Clara standing on a soapbox making a speech. "There's your mother!" the friend said with admiration. But Martha wished her mother was at home waiting for her with milk and cookies, like her friend's mother was! When Martha grew up, however, she became a fighter for social justice just like Clara. She fought for the rights of nurses, longshoremen, office workers, farmworkers, and teachers. She fought against racial prejudice.

Rita thought she got more attention from her mother because she was the youngest. But she hated Wednesdays. On Wednesdays Clara washed the sheets and hung them to dry. Then she went into Manhattan for an organizational meeting, so Rita came home to an empty apartment—and had to make all the beds herself! Rita also grew up to fight for people, especially in the area of fair housing. She always loved to read, just like her mother. And although she understood why Clara was important, and even famous, she always thought of her just as a wonderful mother.

Clara doted on her grandchildren and they adored her. She loved to bake, and her grandchildren loved to eat her blintzes, and her rugelach, a traditional Jewish pastry. One time she baked a batch of rugelach with a great-niece and then demanded they hide the cookies around the apartment so the family wouldn't eat them all at once!

Clara was an example in the way she lived her everyday life. She believed in healthy living: she ate good, healthful food and exercised every day. She had a routine: deep knee bends, touching her toes, jumping jacks. She even exercised her face muscles by standing in front of a mirror and saying, "I am beautiful. I am lover-ly."

But most importantly, Clara's grandchildren say that she is the person they measure themselves to. *What would Clara say? What would Clara do? Does my life have a purpose?*

They remember that wherever she went, Clara talked to workers. She asked about their jobs. *Do they get paid well enough? Do the bosses give them enough breaks? What happens when they get sick or need to take care of sick family?* She gave them advice if she didn't like the answers.

When Clara was very old, and couldn't take care of herself anymore, she went to live in a nursing home where she could be taken care of. Clara being Clara, she looked around her nursing home and asked the workers her usual questions. Then she encouraged them to form a union.

She told the staff that they should serve fresh fruit, because it is good for you. But not grapes! Why? During that time, grape pickers were trying to form a union under their leader César Chávez. People were asked to boycott grapes in support of the workers. The nursing home stopped serving grapes!

Clara died in 1982, when she was ninety-six years old. Her persistence made a difference in laws about how workers are treated today. And people who fight for workers' rights today are inspired by Clara. There are awards named for Clara. The Clara Lemlich Public Service Award is given out by the Triangle Shirtwaist Factory Fire Memorial. And the Clara Lemlich Award honors women in their eighties, nineties, and one hundreds "whose brilliant activism has made real and lasting change in the world." Just like Clara.

Clara Lemlich didn't want attention on *herself*. She wanted attention focused on the *causes* she was fighting for. She might not even want this book about her.

But she would want you to try to make the world a better place. She would tell you not to do it alone. And she would want you to know that you can make a difference now. You don't have to wait until you are older.

If you see something wrong, you could ask yourself, *What would Clara say? What would Clara do?*

Clara Lemlich had a dream that all people deserve a good life. She had a fire inside her to make that dream come true. She never gave up. She persisted. You should, too!

HOW YOU CAN PERSIST

by Deborah Heiligman

To honor Clara's voice and her spirit and her persistence, you should:

1. Speak up whenever you see something wrong.

2. Get other people to help you fight for good.

3. Eat well and exercise.

4. Be friendly to all people.

5. Think of the people who made your clothes and say thank you every time you get dressed.

6. Ask your parents to buy clothes from companies that treat their workers fairly.

7. Tell people about Clara Lemlich and her fight for justice and equality and a good life for all people.

8. Stand in front of the mirror every day and tell yourself, "I am beautiful. I am lover-ly." Repeat five times!

ACKNOWLEDGMENTS

I would like to thank Chelsea Clinton for letting me write about this amazing woman, Clara Lemlich. What an inspiration it was to delve into her life. And thank you to everyone at Penguin/Philomel who helped make this book and this series possible: Jill Santopolo, Talia Benamy, Ken Wright, Ellice Lee, Monique Sterling, Shanta Newlin, Shara Hardeson, Krista Ahlberg.

This book would not be what it is without Clara's wonderful family. Thank you to Rita Shavelson Margules for sharing memories of her mother with me. And to Clara's grandchildren who shared their precious memories of and thoughts about Clara—and then, over the course of months, texted, emailed, and called to answer my questions. Talking with each of them helped me know Clara in a way that I couldn't have otherwise. I'm so grateful to: Julia Velson, Joe Velson, Joel Schaffer, David Margules, Adela Margules, and Jane Margules. Many years ago, Joel interviewed family and taped those interviews. He also taped Clara's memorial service. They are housed at Cornell University. But I was writing this book during the COVID-19 lockdown, and that archive was closed. As fortune would have it, Jane had copies of those tapes and happens to live four blocks away from me. She lent them to me, and so I was able to listen to them! Thank you both! Thanks also to Elena Engel for sharing her memories of her great-aunt and her relationship with Ella (her sister). Thank you also for Clara's rugalach recipe, which I've shared on my website.

A special thank-you to my children and their partners for their input and especially for their inspiration. While I was writing this book, Sarah was organizing a union at her company, Katie was running for political office, Benjamin was fighting for change, and Aaron was finding a new job to help save the world. We now ask each other: What would Clara do?

My agent, Susan Ginsburg, is an invaluable ally and friend and someone who is not afraid to speak her mind—and also always looks terrific. Clara would have loved her!

I am grateful to all my friends and family, and a very special thank-you to my husband, Jonathan, who was right next to me, as always, with support, cheer, advice, love, and a delicious cup of coffee every morning.

ᴄ *References* ᴄ

PRIMARY SOURCES

Lemlich, Clara. "The Inside of a Shirtwaist
Factory: An Appeal to Women Who Wear
Choice and Beautiful Clothing." *Good
Housekeeping*, Volume 54, Issue 3, March 1912.

Lemlich, Clara. "Miss Clara Lemlich, Shirt-Waist
Maker, Replies to New York Senator on
Relieving Working Women of the Burden and

Responsibility of Life." Wage Earner's Suffrage
League, n.d.

Lemlich, Clara. Edited by Morris U. Schappes.
"Remembering the Waistmakers General Strike,
1909," *Jewish Currents*, November 1982.

INTERVIEWS

Joel Schaffer, Clara's grandson, conducted
interviews with members of the family and
friends in the 1970s. He also recorded Clara's
memorial service. I listened to a copy of
these tapes, which are permanently housed
at the Kheel Center for Labor-Management
Documentation & Archives, Cornell
University Library. rmc.library.cornell.edu
/EAD/htmldocs/KCL06131av.html.

TELEPHONE INTERVIEWS WITH THE AUTHOR,
CONDUCTED SUMMER OF 2020, AS WELL AS
FOLLOW-UP INTERVIEWS AND EMAILS

Engel, Elena, great-niece of Clara Lemlich
    Shavelson.

Margules, Adela, Clara's granddaughter.

Margules, David, Clara's grandson.

Margules, Jane, Clara's granddaughter.

Margules, Rita Shavelson, Clara's daughter.

Schaffer, Joel, Clara's grandson.

Velson, Joe, Clara's grandson.

Velson, Julia, Clara's granddaughter.

BOOKS

Markel, Michelle, and Melissa Sweet,

   illustrator. *Brave Girl: Clara and the*

   Shirtwaist Makers' Strike of 1909. New York:

   Balzer + Bray, 2013.

Orleck, Annelise. *Common Sense and a Little*

   Fire: Women and Working-Class Politics in

   the United States, 1900–1965. Chapel Hill:

   The University of North Carolina Press,

   1995.

Tax, Meredith. *The Rising of the Women: Feminist Solidarity and Class Conflict 1880–1917*. Urbana, IL: University of Illinois Press, 2001.

Von Drehle, David. *Triangle: The Fire that Changed America*. New York: Atlantic Monthly Press, 2003.

ARTICLES

Greenberg, Zoe. "Overlooked No More: Clara Lemlich Shavelson, Crusading Leader of Labor Rights." *The New York Times*, August 1, 2018. nytimes.com/2018/08/01/obituaries /overlooked-clara-lemlich-shavelson.html.

ILGWU News-History. "Waistermakers
Vote General Strike." Fiftieth Anniversary
Convention Issue, Chapter 3: 1909–10.
Broadside.

Scheier, Paula. "Clara Lemlich Shavelson:
50 Years in Labor's Front Line." *Jewish Life*,
November 1954.

WEBSITES

clara.commons.gc.cuny.edu/about

jwa.org/encyclopedia/article/shavelson-clara-lemlich

laborarts.org/lemlichawards/2020

labormovement.blogs.brynmawr.edu/1910/04/07

  /interview-with-clara-lemlich

pbs.org/wgbh/americanexperience/features

  /biography-clara-lemlich

wams.nyhistory.org/modernizing-america

  /fighting-for-social-reform/clara-lemlich

VIDEOS

Bitzer, G. W. *Arrival of Emigrants [i.e.,*

  Immigrants], Ellis Island. United States:

  American Mutoscope and Biograph Company,

  1906. From Library of Congress. Video.

  www.loc.gov/item/00694368.

Bonine, R. *Lower Broadway*. United States:
American Mutoscope and Biograph
Company, 1902. From Library of Congress.
Video. loc.gov/item/00694372.

Muttreja, Ashima, and Rebecca Hazell. "Well,
We Showed Them." From Cornell University
Library. Video. ecommons.cornell.edu
/handle/1813/12592.

DEBORAH HEILIGMAN is the author of over thirty books, most of them nonfiction, including *Torpedoed: The True Story of the World War II Sinking of "The Children's Ship," Vincent and Theo: The Van Gogh Brothers, Charles and Emma: The Darwins' Leap of Faith*, and *The Boy Who Loved Math: The Improbable Life of Paul Erdos*. Her books have won the SCBWI Golden Kite Award, the YALSA Excellence in Nonfiction Award, the *Boston Globe–Horn Book* Award for nonfiction, and the ALA Printz Honor, and they've been longlisted for the National Book Awards and been featured on the *New York Times* notable books list. She lives in New York City with her husband and their dog, Zuzu.

You can visit Deborah Heiligman online at
deborahheiligman.com
or follow her on Twitter and Instagram
@DHeiligman

GILLIAN FLINT has worked as a professional illustrator since earning an animation and illustration degree in 2003. Her work has since been published in the UK, USA and Australia. In her spare time, Gillian enjoys reading, spending time with her family and puttering about in the garden on sunny days. She lives in the northwest of England.

You can visit Gillian Flint online at
gillianflint.com
or follow her on Twitter
@GillianFlint
and on Instagram
@gillianflint_illustration

CHELSEA CLINTON is the author of the #1 *New York Times* bestseller *She Persisted: 13 American Women Who Changed the World*; *She Persisted Around the World: 13 Women Who Changed History*; *She Persisted in Sports: American Olympians Who Changed the Game*; *Don't Let Them Disappear: 12 Endangered Species Across the Globe*; *It's Your World: Get Informed, Get Inspired & Get Going!*; *Start Now!: You Can Make a Difference*; with Hillary Clinton, *Grandma's Gardens* and *Gutsy Women*; and, with Devi Sridhar, *Governing Global Health: Who Runs the World and Why?* She is also the Vice Chair of the Clinton Foundation, where she works on many initiatives, including those that help empower the next generation of leaders. She lives in New York City with her husband, Marc, their children and their dog, Soren.

You can follow Chelsea Clinton on Twitter
@ChelseaClinton
or on Facebook at
facebook.com/chelseaclinton

ALEXANDRA BOIGER has illustrated nearly twenty picture books, including the She Persisted books by Chelsea Clinton; the popular Tallulah series by Marilyn Singer; and the Max and Marla books, which she also wrote. Originally from Munich, Germany, she now lives outside of San Francisco, California, with her husband, Andrea, daughter, Vanessa, and two cats, Luiso and Winter.

You can visit Alexandra Boiger online at
alexandraboiger.com
or follow her on Instagram
@alexandra_boiger

Don't miss the rest of the books in the

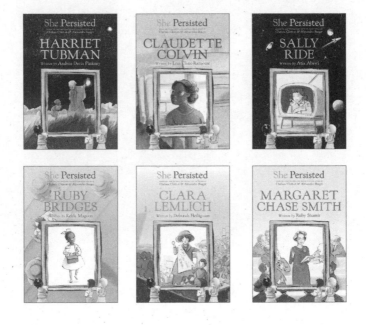

She Persisted series!